Where is the Serengeti?

by Nico Medina

illustrated by Manuel Gutierrez

Penguin Workshop

For the Hamilton cubs: Cameron, Colin,
and Cooper—NM

Para vos—MG

PENGUIN WORKSHOP
An Imprint of Penguin Random House LLC, New York

Visit us online at www.penguinrandomhouse.com.

Library of Congress Cataloging-in-Publication Data is available upon request.

ISBN 9781524792565 (paperback)   10 9 8 7 6 5 4 3 2 1
ISBN 9781524792572 (library binding)   10 9 8 7 6 5 4 3 2 1

Contents

Where Is the Serengeti?

The lioness approaches the herd of wildebeests in plain sight. If she were hunting the wildebeests, she would crouch low and disappear into the tall grass. Her tan coat would help camouflage the lioness. (*Camouflage* means to blend in with her surroundings.)

But for right now, she's only watching the herd.

And the herd watches her back. Nervously. The wildebeests walk on, all the while keeping an eye on the female lion.

The lioness can't outrun the wildebeests. In short bursts, lions can reach speeds of fifty miles per hour. But wildebeests can run that fast for a long time. So if the lioness is far away from the herd, the wildebeests will be safe. And if the lioness decides to charge them, they'll have plenty of time to run for their lives.

The lioness walks alongside the herd. Lions prefer to attack when their target is no more than a hundred feet away. With a good running start, they can leap as far as thirty-six feet! But this lioness doesn't want the wildebeests to panic and

run—at least not yet. For now, she wants to keep their attention on her. Slowly, she begins closing the distance between them.

The wildebeests notice, and turn to flee.

The lioness charges, running straight for the herd!

She's too far back. She'll never catch up.

But on the other side of the herd, lying in wait in the tall grass, are two more lionesses. And the panicked wildebeests are running right toward them.

Suddenly, the other lionesses spring into action. They jump up into a run and select their target: a lone wildebeest that has separated from the herd.

The lioness that reaches the wildebeest first sinks her claws into its backside. The wildebeest bucks in an attempt to shake the lioness off, but it's no use.

The wildebeest is one of the largest species—or types—of antelope, weighing up to six hundred pounds. But the lioness is strong. The wildebeest is pulled to the ground. Now a second lioness arrives and delivers the killing blow: a sure and swift bite to the throat.

The wildebeest's death may seem brutal. But lions and their cubs need meat to survive. Predators, like lions, must hunt and kill prey, like wildebeests.

As the lions feast on their fresh kill, smaller carnivores (meat eaters), like jackals, wait in the background. Vultures circle overhead. After the lions have had their fill, the jackals and the vultures will swarm in to fight over the scraps. Soon, the wildebeest's bones will be picked clean.

When survival is at stake, nothing goes to waste.

This is life in the Serengeti (say: sair-en-GET-ee), a wide, grassy plain in the east-central African nation of Tanzania. Serengeti National Park was established in 1951. It covers an area of 5,700 square miles—about the size of Connecticut.

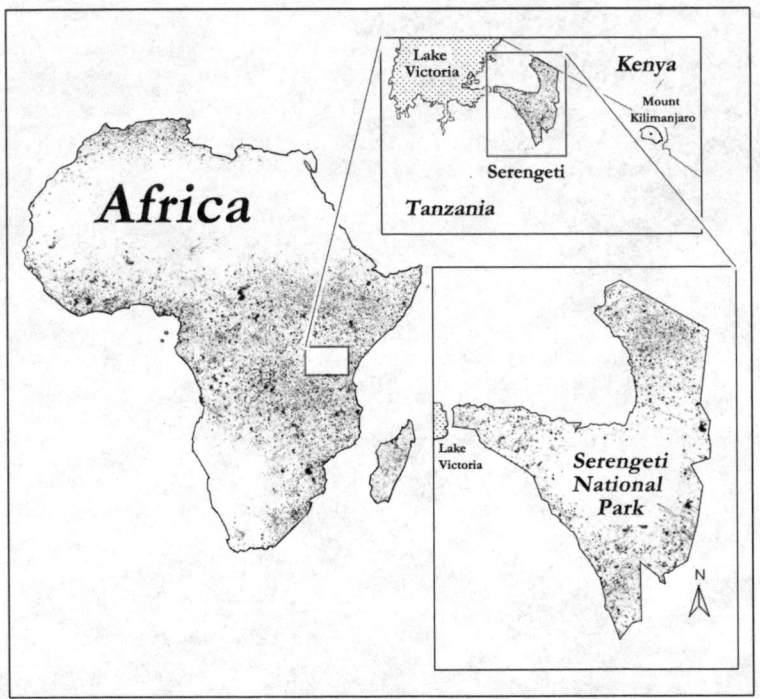

Soon after the park was founded, elephants began moving back to the Serengeti. They had not been in the area for many years, having been driven out by hunters. Today, there are thousands of elephants on the Serengeti Plain. The area is also home to as many as two million wildebeests, four thousand lions, and a wide variety of other animals, including zebras, gazelles, giraffes, leopards, and hyenas.

With all these animals, the Serengeti holds the highest concentration of large game and predators on earth. (That means the greatest number of these animals are living in the smallest area.)

In 1981, the Serengeti was named a World Heritage Site by the United Nations. It is a place "of outstanding universal value" to humankind. The Grand Canyon in the United States and the Great Barrier Reef in Australia are other World Heritage Sites.

Today, no people—except for a few scientists

and park rangers—are allowed to live in Serengeti
National Park. It is a wild and special place,
practically untouched by humans, and ruled by
great beasts.

CHAPTER 1
Endless Plains and Mountain Islands

In the language of the local Maasai people (say: ma-SIGH), *Serengeti* means "endless plains" or "extended place." The Maasai arrived here from Kenya, to the north, about three hundred years ago. They used the grasslands to graze their cattle.

Maasai women

There are around two hundred species of grass on the Serengeti Plain. There are short grasslands in the south and east, with taller grasslands in the west. Millions of animals—wildebeests, zebras,

buffalo—graze here. A single elephant can eat six hundred pounds of grass in a day! The Serengeti's vegetation feeds the largest herds of animals on the planet.

To the north and west is the savanna, grasslands with trees here and there. Some areas of the savanna are more heavily forested. Here, only giraffes can feed on the tallest leaves in the trees. A number of small rivers, lakes, and swamps dot the park.

The Serengeti lies just a couple of hundred miles south of the equator. The equator is an imaginary line that divides the earth into northern and southern halves.

Areas around the equator receive more year-round direct sunlight than anywhere else on the planet. These places don't experience four distinct seasons—winter, spring, summer, and fall—like other areas around the world.

There are basically two seasons in the Serengeti: a rainy one and a dry one. During the rainy season, from about October through May, it might rain twenty-two days in a month. Around thirty-three inches of rain will fall during the rainy season.

From June to September, it rains only about five inches total—with as few as six rainy days each month.

Areas in the northern Serengeti are the wettest, with about fifty-five inches of annual rainfall. The southeastern short-grass plains are the driest.

A mother cheetah and her cubs

The Serengeti is a high plain—between three thousand and six thousand feet above sea level. Because of this, temperatures can get a bit cool at night—between 57° and 61° Fahrenheit—even though the Serengeti is so close to the equator. During the day, temperatures can rise into the mid-eighties.

While the Serengeti Plain is mostly flat, there are some hilly areas. "Mountain islands" of granite rock in a sea of grass also dot the landscape. They are called kopjes (sounds like "copies") and can be hundreds of feet tall.

Kopjes are like their own little ecosystems within the larger savanna ecosystem. (An ecosystem is a community of living things within an area, or environment.) These rocky mounds attract a wide variety of life.

Rainwater collects in the rock hollows. Plants and bushes that can't survive among the grasses are able to grow in kopjes by taking root in their

The Moru Kopjes in Serengeti National Park

cracks and crevices. Small animals like snakes, lizards, and mice—drawn to the kopjes by little pools of drinking water—make their home here.

The dik-dik, one of the world's smallest antelopes, is one animal that can be found living around kopjes. These tiny animals stand only about a foot high and weigh up to fifteen pounds. Females are larger than males. Male dik-diks grow tiny horns—only about three inches long!

Dik-diks live in pairs rather than a herd, and they mate for life. To mark their territory, dik-diks rub their faces in the grass. This releases a sticky fluid from a black spot in the corner of the dik-dik's eyes. So it's almost like they use tears to set the boundaries of their home!

Kopjes also make great lookouts for larger predators like cheetahs and leopards. From atop a kopje, these big cats can spot prey miles across the savanna. And before leaving to hunt, the cat can hide her cubs in the kopje's rocky burrows. (Of course, these predators also hunt the small animals that live around the kopjes!)

One unusual little creature that makes kopjes its home is the rock hyrax.

While the ten-pound rock hyrax might look like a prairie dog or guinea pig, it is actually related to the elephant! Like an elephant, the hyrax has tusks and flat, hoof-like nails. One of its toes has a long nail that is used for grooming and scratching.

Rock hyraxes live in Africa and the Middle East, in large groups of up to eighty individuals. They spend most of their time relaxing, lying on top of one another in heaps in their dens or out in the sunlight.

Rock hyrax   Guinea pig

Of course, the hyraxes must remain vigilant. Lookouts keep watch for predators. When danger appears, it's time to sound the alarm. Hyraxes have a kind of "language," with more than twenty different noises—from grunts to growls to snorts. Male hyraxes actually sing "songs" using patterns of these sounds to let other hyraxes in the area know: *Hey—keep out of our kopje!* The songs help to protect their territory.

CHAPTER 2
From Ashes to Grasses

From the tiny mouse to the enormous elephant, how can the Serengeti support so much life?

How did the Serengeti become this way?

It all began with the formation of the Great Rift Valley.

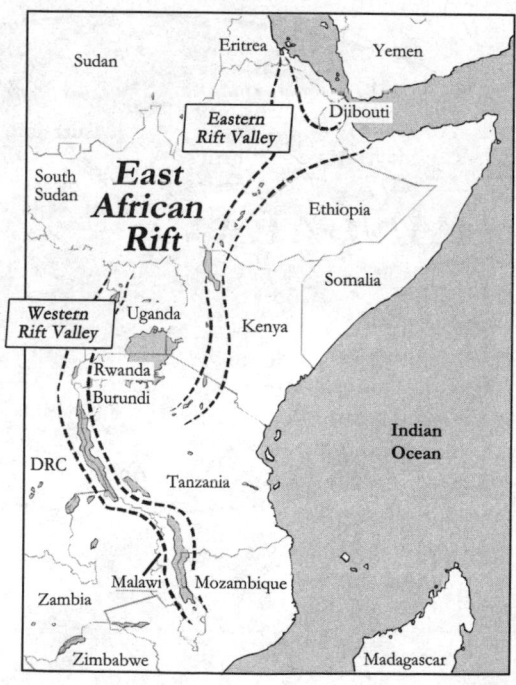

Great Rift Valley

Continents on the Move!

The surface of our planet, also known as the earth's crust, is always in motion. That's because the crust is made of many different plates, and these plates move in all directions. But they move very *slowly*—four inches per year, tops! Three hundred million years ago, there was only one continent—

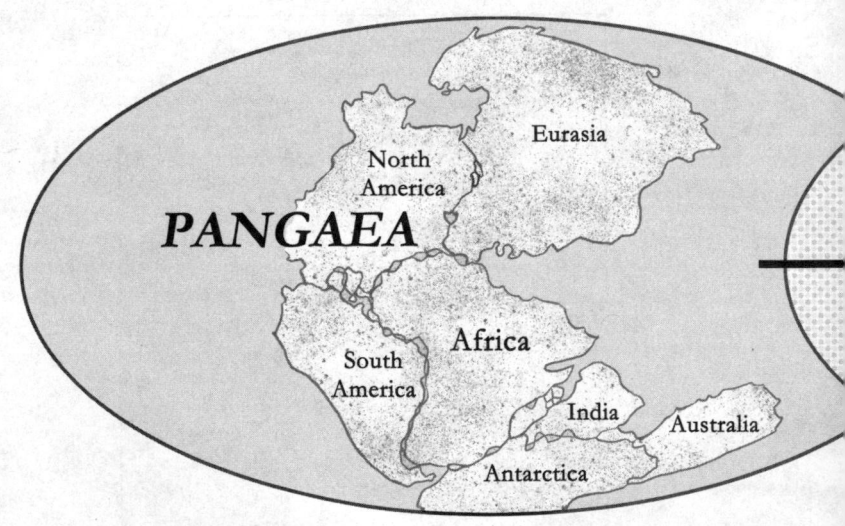

a supercontinent called Pangaea (say: pan-JEE-uh). Over millions of years, Pangaea broke apart into the different continents we know today. Africa's Great Rift Valley formed as the African Plate began to split in two. Earthquakes and volcanoes occur at the meeting place of different plates, including the Great Rift Valley.

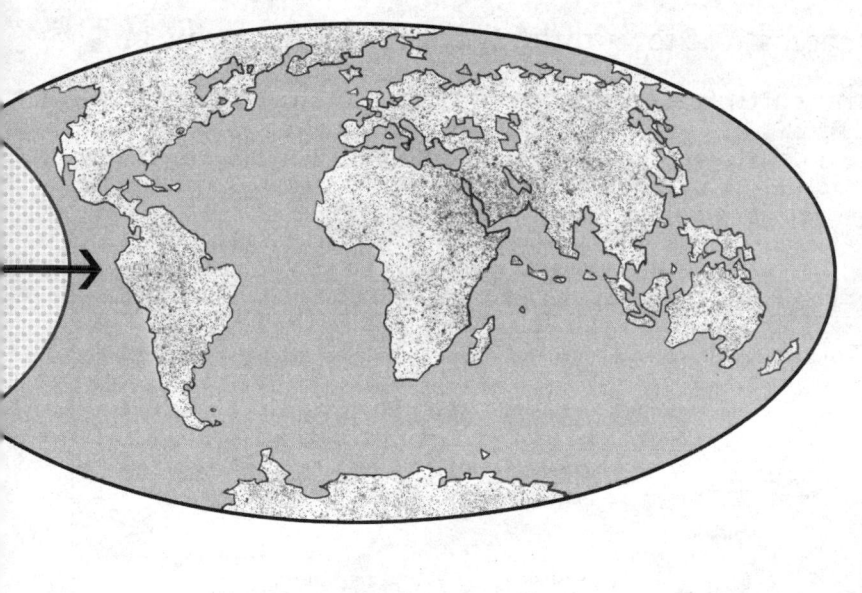

More than twenty million years ago, the African continent began to split up. As East Africa and West Africa drifted apart, the earth's surface between them weakened. The land began to crack and tear. Eventually, a long gash in the earth opened up: the Great Rift Valley. The valley runs from southeast Africa to the Middle East—more than three thousand miles!

As the earth's crust weakened and the Great Rift Valley deepened, a thick molten hot liquid called magma rose toward the surface. Magma forms in the earth's mantle. That's the layer just beneath the crust. When magma breaks the surface of the earth, it is called lava.

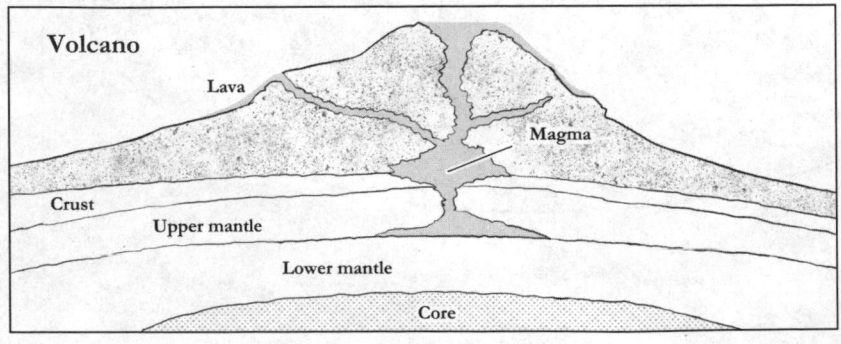

24

Volcanoes formed. They erupted violently, sending hot lava ash flying high into the sky. This ash settled over the Serengeti Plain. Over millions of years, it turned into a rich soil, perfect for growing grasses.

Ol Doinyo Lengai

Today, there is just one active volcano in the area. The rest are dormant. They don't erupt. Ol Doinyo Lengai, or "Mountain of the God" in the Maasai language, stands more than ten thousand feet high. The lava that erupts from this volcano turns white when it meets the air. When it rains, the ash becomes hard as concrete.

Volcanic activity beneath the earth's crust also led to the formation of the Serengeti's kopjes. Five hundred million years ago, well before the age of dinosaurs, hot liquid bubbles of granite began to rise up from the earth's mantle. As they reached the crust, they hardened into solid rock, with softer rock formed around it. Over time, the softer rock began to wear away from rain

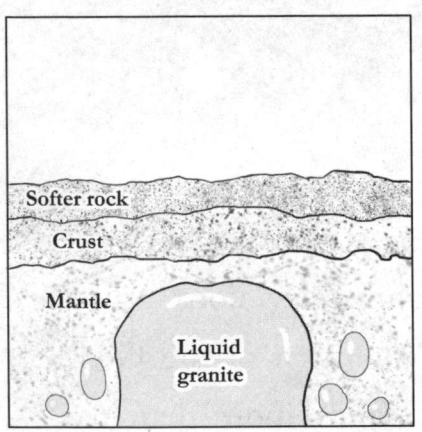
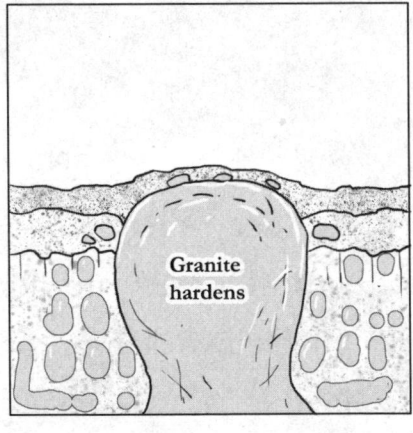

and wind. What are left over today are the granite kopjes.

The Serengeti owes its fertile plains and rich variety of life to these ancient volcanic forces. The Serengeti Plain supports enormous herds of different animals, which in turn feed thousands of predators.

But as lush as its grasslands can be, when the rains stop, the Serengeti's grasses begin to disappear. And when the great herds' pastures dry up, they must move on—they must migrate— in search of food and water.

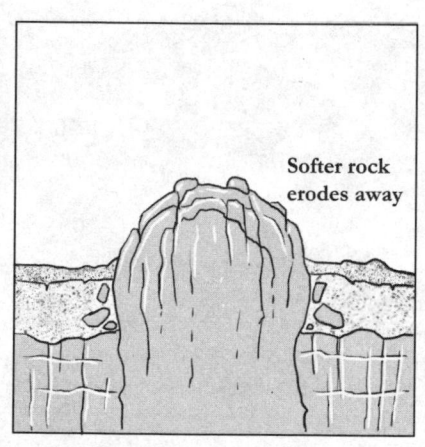

Softer rock erodes away

Kopje

Ngorongoro Crater: Life in a Bowl

Near the Serengeti lies another protected land, called Ngorongoro (say: nn-GOR-un-GOR-oh). It was named a World Heritage Site by the United Nations in 1979.

Ngorongoro Crater is the world's largest caldera, or volcanic depression. It was formed 2.5 million years ago, when a giant volcano collapsed on itself after a major eruption. The crater is two thousand feet deep and twelve miles across. Its rim is lined

with dense forests; its floor is lush grassland.

One hundred square miles in area—about the size of Orlando, Florida—Ngorongoro Crater is its own little paradise. Lakes dot the landscape, and there is plenty of water year-round. Because of this, the herds of wildebeests and zebras that live here don't need to migrate. But some animals migrate *to* the crater from very far away. Ngorongoro's lakes attract thousands of birds—from flamingos from southwest Africa to white storks from Europe and Asia.

CHAPTER 3
The Great Wildebeest Migration

Besides the majestic African lion, the wildebeest—also known as the gnu (sounds like "new")—is the true symbol of the Serengeti.

Some people joke that these funny-looking members of the antelope family were put together

Wildebeest

from the spare parts of other animals. Long, horselike face. Small set of horns. Shaggy beard. Bushy mane.

But while wildebeests may look a little strange, they rule the grassy plains. There are two million of these ungulates (say: UN-gyoo-lets) in the Serengeti. (Ungulates are animals that have hooves.) Wildebeests here outnumber all the zebras, gazelles, buffalo, giraffes, and warthogs combined—and then some.

Ungulates

From January to March, about half a million wildebeests are born on the southern Serengeti plains. This spectacular event ensures that the wildebeest herd will survive another year.

Calves weigh about forty-five pounds at birth. They are born with a yellowish-brown hide that darkens to look like the adults within a couple of months. Wildebeest calves will drink their mother's milk for six to nine months, but they are also able to eat grass within two weeks.

After about three years, the calves will be fully grown—up to eight feet long, six hundred pounds, with horns measuring three feet across. While not every calf survives till adulthood, many of them do—and will have calves of their own. Wildebeests can live up to twenty years in the wild.

Calving season on the savanna attracts many predators. Young wildebeests are a favorite prey of the spotted hyena. So wildebeest calves need to be able to stand up on their own four hooves within minutes of being born. And within a few days, they must keep pace with their mother. Because in March, the herds will leave the southern plains.

The Great Wildebeest Migration is about to begin. Between now and the next calving season in January, the wildebeests will travel for five hundred miles in one giant circle, in search of food and water. It is the world's longest overland animal migration.

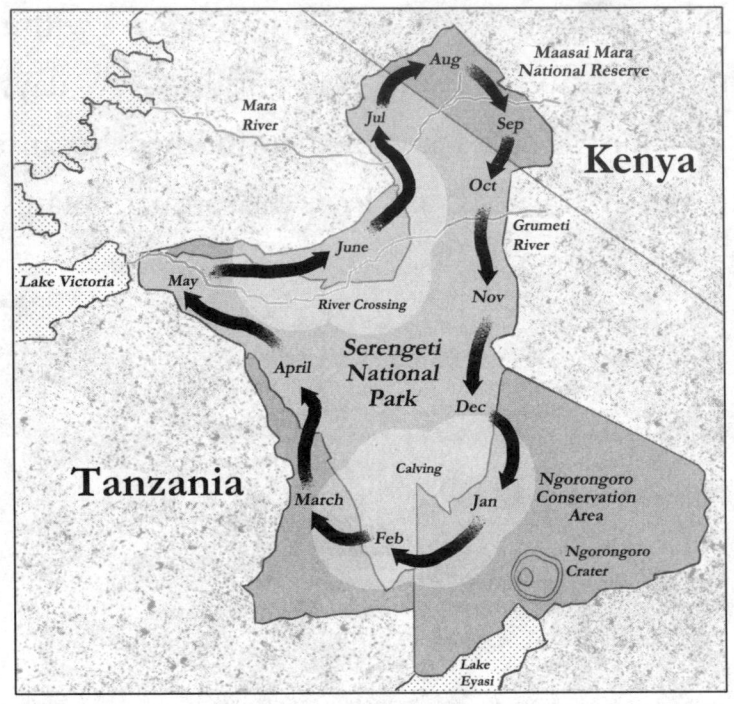

Great Wildebeest Migration

Other animals join the migration as well, including a great number of zebras. The wildebeests don't mind, because zebras and wildebeests eat different parts of the Serengeti's grasses. Plus, zebras have better eyesight than wildebeests, and wildebeests hear better than zebras. Their different skills come in handy when keeping an eye—or an ear—out for predators.

The plains zebra is the most common of the three species of zebra. They can be as tall as five feet at the shoulder and weigh nine hundred pounds.

Plains zebras

Zebras have white coats with black stripes. But under those white coats, zebras' skin is actually black!

When zebras crowd together, their stripes make it difficult for predators to focus on one individual animal. This is particularly good protection against lions.

A zebra's stripes also help protect it against biting insects. That's because the bugs are more attracted to animals whose coats are one solid, easy-to-spot color.

Thomson's gazelles (sometimes called Tommys) and eland are two members of the antelope family

Thomson's gazelles

Eland

that are also welcome along on the wildebeests'
migration. Less than four feet long and weighing
around fifty pounds, gazelles are a favorite prey of
the cheetah. Eland are the largest antelope on the
Serengeti and can weigh more than two thousand
pounds.

In March, the wildebeests and their calves leave the short-grass plains of the south. Traveling in huge groups that can stretch on for twenty-five miles, they follow the rains to the north and west into the long-grass plains.

By June, the rains stop. This is the wildebeests' mating season. By the time they have eaten all the grass available, nine out of every ten female wildebeests will be pregnant.

As the grasslands begin to die and dry up, the herds must move once again in search of food and water. They must press on through heat, thirst, and hunger until they find them. But without rain clouds to follow, how do they know where to go?

Instinct tells the herds to head north, to the Maasai Mara plains. (Instinct is something that is understood naturally, rather than learned. Think of how a newborn baby knows *by instinct* to drink its mother's milk.) There will be plenty of grass on the Maasai Mara. But to get there, the herds must cross the Grumeti and Mara Rivers, where deadly dangers await them.

The Nile crocodile can grow up to twenty feet long and weigh more than 1,500 pounds. However, they never truly stop growing . . . until they die. They can live up to seventy years in the wild.

This skilled predator has been around for millions of years and has changed very little since prehistoric times. Nile crocs once hunted the dinosaurs. Today, they hunt wildebeests. For the Nile crocodile, the Great Wildebeest Migration is more like the Great Wildebeest *Feast*!

As the herds gather on the riverbank, the crocs lie in wait in the muddy brown water. Their thick, leathery scales help them blend into the river perfectly. Only their eyes, ears, and nostrils poke out from beneath the surface, so they can take in the scene without giving themselves away.

Instinct tells the wildebeests to be cautious. They know that danger lurks in the river even if they can't detect the hidden crocs. Sometimes the nervous herds wait at the riverbank for days before finally taking the plunge and crossing the river. But the crocodiles are in no rush. And the larger ones can go for a year without a meal—so waiting a couple of extra days is no big deal!

Eventually, the need to push on with the journey urges the first wildebeest into the water. The rest follow. There is safety in numbers.

But not all will be lucky.

The crocodiles watch until their meals are within striking distance. Once a croc snags a wildebeest in its superstrong jaws, it drags its victim below the surface, drowning it.

The crocs' sixty to seventy sharp, cone-shaped teeth are built for biting down on prey. Their jaws can't move sideways, which means they can't chew their food. So crocs use a "death roll"—twisting their bodies around in circles—to rip off bite-size pieces, which are swallowed whole. Sometimes crocs will help each other pull apart an animal.

While many wildebeests will die in the jaws of a crocodile, for each one a croc captures, fifty more die of drowning. The riverbanks can be steep, narrow, and slippery. Some animals are trampled to death during the herd's panicked river crossing.

Those that survive may have broken legs and be unable to climb up the riverbank. Stuck, they may die from exhaustion—or as a lion's meal.

All told, about 250,000 wildebeests will die each year during the migration. More than 6,000 die while crossing the Mara River.

As harsh as this may seem, mass wildebeest drownings provide tons of dead meat for animals like vultures, storks, fish, crocodiles, and hyenas.

Insects lay their eggs in the rotting carcasses—when they hatch, the maggots will provide food for still *more* animals. Even after all the meat has been picked off, the bones will leach nutrients into the river for up to seven years. Algae and bacteria grow on and around them, feeding the river's catfish.

By now it is July or August. The herds make their final push into the Maasai Mara plains, just across the Tanzania-Kenya border. The Maasai

Mara is not part of the Serengeti, but the herds will find miles and miles of pasture here. They will graze in the Maasai Mara for months.

When the rains return in October and November, the great herds will follow the rains south, back to the Serengeti Plain, completing the circular migration that began nearly a year earlier.

CHAPTER 4
The Pride

For every lion on the Serengeti, there are about *five hundred* wildebeests. Other big cats—leopards, cheetahs, tigers, cougars—are solitary creatures. But lions are social. Lions live in large groups called prides. They greet each other with nuzzles and rubs, much like a house cat rubs against its human.

A pride is typically made up of about a dozen lionesses, up to three males, and the pride's cubs. The female cubs that survive to adulthood usually stay with the pride, but the males will leave to try to form their own prides. Or take over another one.

When a male lion challenges another, it can sometimes be a fight to the death. And when a new male comes into a pride, he will kill all the cubs. Lions are also known to kill rival predators and their young—like leopards and cheetahs.

Hunting Cheetahs

Cheetahs are the fastest land animals on earth, reaching speeds of seventy miles per hour in seconds! Five thousand years ago, people in ancient Sumer (present-day Iraq) used cheetahs as hunters. While on a hunt, the cheetah was kept blindfolded until prey was in sight. Then the cat's handler would remove the blindfold and release the animal to run down its victim. The practice of keeping hunting cheetahs spread. Akbar the Great, an emperor in India in the 1500s, kept as many as nine thousand cheetahs over the course of his life!

A painting of a cheetah hunt from the 1600s

Only male lions have manes—a circle of long hair around the head. The fuller and darker the mane, the healthier and stronger the lion. Males guard the pride's land. While on patrol, they roar as if to tell any would-be intruders: *Keep away.* A lion's roar can be heard from five miles away.

Male lions can weigh more than four hundred pounds and stand nearly four feet high at the shoulder. Lionesses are a bit shorter and weigh up to three hundred pounds.

While male lions may be bigger and stronger, females do up to 90 percent of the pride's hunting. And they prefer to hunt at night. Their eyes are six times more sensitive to light than humans' eyes, so they see very well in the dark. When they hunt during the day, they fail more often than they succeed.

Males will sometimes join the hunt in order to bring down larger prey, like Cape buffalo. But no matter who's doing the hunting, the male lions get to eat first, followed by the lionesses and their cubs.

Cape Buffalo

Weighing in at close to two thousand pounds, the Cape buffalo is a force to be reckoned with. They live in herds, and when threatened by predators, the adults will form a protective circle around their young. A male Cape buffalo's horns can measure up to forty inches across, with a thick bony plate covering its forehead. These sharp horns are deadly weapons. Unlike most game, Cape buffalo will charge at human hunters—sometimes without warning.

While lions will sometimes hunt alone, they do better in a group. A pride's survival depends on cooperation. Females even help one another to nurse and raise their young. There is no single leader in a pride; they work as a team.

Sometimes the team has to defend their territory against rival lions. For a lion pride, some land is more desirable than other land. For example, it is good to have a river or a watering hole in the pride's territory, because prey will be drawn to the drinking water.

But it's not only rival prides that lions have to worry about. The spotted hyena—another predator that lives in large social groups—is the lion's fiercest competitor on the Serengeti. And it can be just as deadly.

CHAPTER 5
Queen Hyena

About 3,500 spotted hyenas live in the Serengeti. Hyenas live in large groups called clans. Hyena clans are larger than lion prides and may include upward of eighty members.

Unlike lions, a hyena clan has a clear leader: the matriarch (say: MAY-tree-ark). That means a female is head of the clan. Female hyenas are larger than the males, weighing up to 190 pounds. And the matriarch is the biggest and most aggressive female in the group. She is queen of the clan, and leads the clan on their hunts.

Female hyena   Male hyena

The queen's rank is passed down to her strongest daughter. Hyena cubs are born black and with their eyes open. As soon as they are born, they begin to fight to show each other who's boss. The less aggressive cubs will get less milk, and may not survive to adulthood.

Hyena cub, about 3.5 pounds

The rest of the female clan members hold different ranks. The lower the rank, the longer that hyena waits to eat. Because of this, cubs belonging to high-ranking clan members will grow bigger and stronger than those whose mother has a lower rank.

Male hyenas rank dead last. Luckily, they can chew and eat bone, because sometimes, that's all they get. Females will attack males who step out of line. Even rowdy female cubs get to pick on them.

US president and naturalist Theodore Roosevelt once said that the hyena was "as cowardly as it is savage." That was because people believed hyenas didn't hunt for themselves but rather stole kills from other predators.

However, a scientist working in the Serengeti in the 1960s found that lions stole more from hyenas than the other way around. Hyenas are highly intelligent creatures, and relationships among the clan members are complex. While doing research in the Ngorongoro Crater, primate expert Jane Goodall once said that hyenas were "second only to chimpanzees in fascination."

Spotted hyenas are sometimes called "laughing

hyenas" because of the distinct giggling sound they make when they're nervous or excited. Each hyena also has its own special "whoop"—a sound it makes to identify itself to the group. The whoop acts like the individual hyena's name or signature.

Like the lion, the hyena is an apex predator—a predator at the top (or apex) of the food chain. Apex predators have no natural enemies—except one another. Lions and hyenas are bitter rivals. They will kill each other on sight if given the chance, especially if they are caught on their enemy's land. A hyena's bite is so strong it can crush bone.

Jane Goodall (1934–)

Jane Goodall was born in London, England, in 1934. She left school when she was eighteen and traveled to Africa. There, in a place called Gombe Stream in western Tanzania—about four hundred miles southwest of the Serengeti—she began to study chimpanzees in the wild.

At first, she made the wild chimps nervous, and they stayed far away from her. Jane had to be patient. After seeing her every day for two years, the chimps finally trusted Jane enough to approach her.

Jane Goodall discovered a lot about chimps over the many years she spent in Gombe Stream National Park. They use tools—like blades of grass for pulling termites out of mounds to eat them. They hug each other for comfort—but they also can be violent, using stones as weapons. Chimps also have a primitive "language" of more than twenty different sounds.

Hyenas hunt the same large animals as lions do, but they will eat just about anything—even rotting flesh. Hyenas will eat from a decaying hippopotamus carcass for months. They are also more resistant to disease than lions and African wild dogs.

Despite their advantages, many hyenas meet violent ends in the jaws of a lion. But strong hyena clans have been known to challenge weak lion prides for territory. In the Serengeti, the struggle for dominance is never-ending.

Sick as a Dog

African wild dogs nearly disappeared from the Serengeti in the early 1990s. It is believed that they were killed by diseases carried by the thousands of domestic dogs living in the surrounding areas.

Also known as the painted dog, wild dogs live in large groups called packs. Packs number from about ten to forty individuals and are led by a dominant male-female couple. African wild dogs are extremely successful hunters. Unlike lions and cheetahs, they can run for long distances without stopping. This helps them to exhaust their prey. The pups are allowed to eat from the kill first, while the adults stand guard. Food is brought to older, sick, or injured members of the pack.

CHAPTER 6
Cradle of Humanity

Between Serengeti National Park and Ngorongoro Crater lies Olduvai Gorge. Thirty miles long, and nearly three hundred feet deep, Olduvai Gorge is sometimes called the Cradle of Humanity. It is where fossils from the earliest human species were first discovered.

Olduvai Gorge

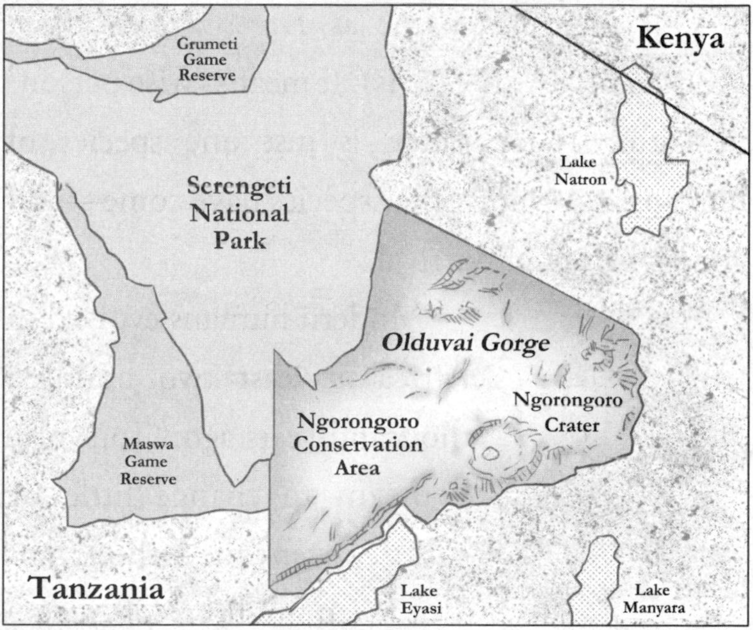

Kenya

Grumeti
Game
Reserve

Lake
Natron

Serengeti
National
Park

Olduvai Gorge

Ngorongoro
Crater

Ngorongoro
Conservation
Area

Maswa
Game
Reserve

Tanzania

Lake
Eyasi

Lake
Manyara

Our scientific name is *Homo sapiens* (say: HOME-oh SAPE-ee-ens). It means "wise person" in Latin. Today, there is just one species of humans: us. Many other species have come—and gone—before our arrival.

Homo habilis

Modern humans evolved in Africa at least two hundred thousand years ago. (To evolve means to change little by little, over time—thousands or even millions of years.) The earliest known human species, *Homo habilis*, lived more than two million years ago.

The first *Homo habilis* fossil was discovered in 1960 in Olduvai Gorge by Mary Leakey and her son Jonathan. After more discoveries and much study, Mary's husband, Louis Leakey, announced their discovery in 1964. *Homo habilis*—meaning "handy man"—were thought to be the first humans to use tools. They were the first to eat meat. They stood around four feet tall and weighed up to seventy pounds.

By the time modern humans evolved, *Homo habilis* was long gone.

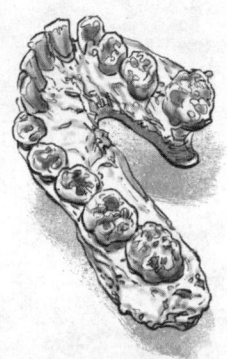

Lower jaw fossil of
Homo habilis

Around seven thousand years ago, a group called the San people lived in what is now Tanzania. The San are thought to be the planet's oldest surviving human tribe.

The San were hunter-gatherers. They used bows and poisoned arrows, snares, and spears to bring down big game.

San people, present day

The Leakeys: First Family of Paleontology

Louis and Mary Leakey

Paleontology is the study of ancient life on earth. The Leakey family is sometimes called the First Family of Paleontology, and with good reason.

Louis Leakey (1903–1972) and Mary Douglas Leakey (1913–1996) first met in England. Louis asked Mary to illustrate his upcoming book about the origins of man. The two also worked together in Olduvai Gorge, where they discovered stone tools and ancient ape fossils. Soon they were married, and in 1937 they moved to Kenya, where they had three sons: Jonathan, who discovered *Homo habilis* with his mother in 1960, and Richard, who discovered another specimen in 1972. (Their third son, Philip, became a member of the Kenyan parliament.) In the late 1970s, Mary discovered fossilized footprints that belonged to an ancient human ancestor even older than *Homo habilis*.

The San lived in groups of three or four families, and there were no real chiefs or leaders. They were nonviolent. So as people from other areas of Africa began to move in, the San were either pushed out or killed. There are about one hundred thousand San people still alive today. They live in southern Africa, far from the Serengeti.

Three thousand years ago, the Cushitic people came to Tanzania from Ethiopia. They introduced farming and agriculture to the area.

Bantu people from the west arrived around the year 500. They brought iron weapons with them. Today, most Tanzanians are of Bantu descent.

Sukuma people, a Bantu ethnic group in Tanzania

The Maasai people arrived in the Serengeti about three hundred years ago. They believed in one god, called Engai. According to the Maasai religion, Engai gave the Maasai all the cattle in the world. Because of this, the Maasai believed all the livestock on earth belonged to them. So as they moved across the Great Rift Valley, they conquered rival tribes and took their cattle.

The Maasai were nomadic, which means they did not live in permanent settlements. Instead, they moved from pasture to pasture with their cattle. They raised livestock not only for meat and milk, but also for blood, which they drank.

The Maasai did not bury anybody except their chieftains. Burial was believed to be bad for the grass. They preferred to leave their dead out on the plains, for the scavengers to eat.

They were fierce warriors. The Maasai weapons of choice were the spear and the *rungu*—a wooden throwing club that could be aimed to hit its target from three hundred feet away.

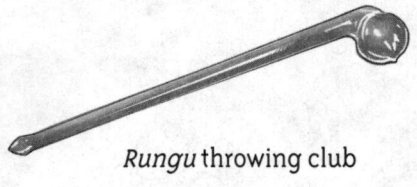

Rungu throwing club

About 1.5 million Maasai still live near the Serengeti today. The governments of Tanzania and Kenya try to encourage them to farm rather than raise livestock.

While the Maasai are less nomadic today

than they were in the past, many have kept their traditional way of life. They live in homes made of mud and cow dung. And they surround their settlements with a fence of thornbushes and use spears—not guns—to protect themselves and their livestock against predators.

Other Maasai people work in the tourism industry, sharing their culture with outsiders.

CHAPTER 7
Safari Hunters

Europeans had been building trading posts and settlements up and down Africa's coastline since the 1400s. But due to fever and disease, and lack of good roads, they did not explore inland for centuries.

That all changed in the mid-1800s. Explorers began to trace Africa's great rivers to their sources. They discovered a land rich in natural resources, including gold, diamonds, and copper. The old legends of Africa's great wealth were proving to be true. And European nations wanted these treasures.

Thus began what is known as the Scramble for Africa. Rather than go to war with one another, the nations of Europe gathered at the Berlin Conference in 1884. They met in the German capital to discuss how to divvy up the African continent among themselves.

Did Africans have a say in what happened to their land? No. Their fate would be decided by foreigners. This was not right.

In the end, Kenya went to Great Britain, and Tanzania went to Germany. The British also controlled Egypt, Sudan, and much of southern Africa. (After World War I, the British would control Tanzania—and the Serengeti—as well.)

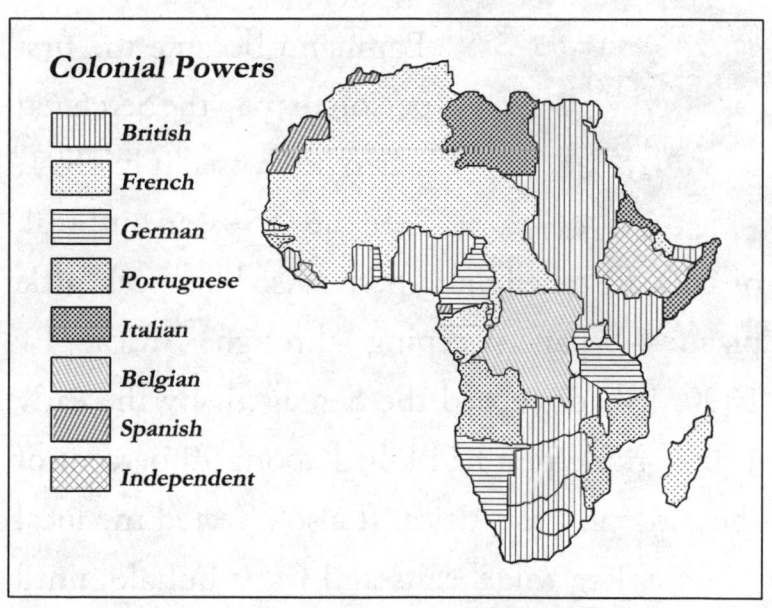

Colonial Powers

British
French
German
Portuguese
Italian
Belgian
Spanish
Independent

Partition of Africa after the Berlin Conference

The rest of the continent was divided among France, Belgium, Spain, Portugal, and Italy. Only two African nations—Liberia and Ethiopia—remained independent after the Scramble.

Oscar Baumann

Over the following years, British settlers began to move inland, toward the Serengeti Plain. An Austrian geographer named Oscar Baumann became the first person to map the Serengeti when he crossed it in 1891.

In the 1880s, an outbreak of a disease called rinderpest—also known as cattle plague—began sweeping through Africa. By 1890, it had reached the Serengeti. By the early 1900s, rinderpest had killed about 90 percent of the cattle in East Africa. It also affected the local wildlife, like wildebeests and Cape buffalo, until the 1960s.

The Maasai were starving. They became weak and desperate. While on his journey across the Serengeti, Oscar Baumann described a tragic scene: "These people ate everything available . . . skins, bones, and even horns of cattle. . . . Swarms of vultures followed them, waiting for victims."

The British convinced the Maasai to sign a series of unfair treaties in 1904 and 1911. These agreements forced the Maasai off their ancestral lands. British settlers wanted the land for their own farms and ranches. More land would be taken from the Maasai in later years.

As the Serengeti became less and less accessible to the Maasai people, the outside world began to "discover" this incredible land for the first time.

In 1913, American writer and hunter Stewart Edward White explored the northern Serengeti. He was amazed by what he saw. His 1915 book *The Rediscovered Country* inspired hunters and adventure-seekers to come to the Serengeti.

Liberia

Ellen Johnson Sirleaf

The West African colony of Liberia was established in 1822 by a group of white Americans who hoped that black American enslaved people would move there after gaining their freedom. Eventually, some thirteen thousand freed American and Caribbean people did just that. In 1847, Liberia declared its independence and became Africa's first republic. Monrovia, named for US president James Monroe, became its capital city.

From 1989 to 2003, Liberians fought two bitter and bloody civil wars; 250,000 lost their lives. Two years later, Liberians elected Ellen Johnson Sirleaf as their president. As Africa's first elected female head of state, Sirleaf worked hard to heal the country after the war.

Today, more than 4.6 million people live in Liberia—roughly the population of Alabama. However, only about 5 percent of Liberians are descended from the freed black people who immigrated there in the 1800s.

White described the vast herds of game he encountered:

"Never have I seen anything like that game. . . . It did not matter in which direction I looked, there it was; as abundant one place as another. . . . And suddenly I realized again that in this beautiful, wide, populous country, no sportsman's rifle has ever been fired."

But because of Stewart Edward White and other sportsmen—who came to be known as "white hunters"—that would change very quickly. *Many* sportsmen's rifles would be fired in the decades to come.

White hunters killed for sport. They led hunting safaris for European and American visitors. The word *safari* (say: suh-FAR-ee) means "journey" or "expedition" in the African Swahili language. Originally, it comes from the Arabic word *sāfara*.

Today, people on safari usually observe and photograph wild animals in their natural habitat. But back in the days of Africa's white hunters, safaris were hunting parties that could last for months, killing off many creatures.

Their main target: lions.

Because lions occasionally preyed on livestock, hunters were encouraged to shoot them on sight. As many as fifty to one hundred lions could be killed on a single safari—lionesses and cubs included. Sometimes safari expeditions recruited local guides and spearmen to help with the hunt.

Some hunters would lure the lions with meat, then shoot them as they approached. One white hunter bragged about all the hyenas he and his safari party had shot in order to attract lions.

But it wasn't just lions that suffered—hunters also targeted other large game, like buffalo, elephants, and leopards. Sometimes they shot at these animals from moving vehicles.

While the overhunting of lions and other animals was hugely damaging to the local wildlife population, it led to one positive outcome: a new conservation movement for the Serengeti.

A Presidential Safari

Safaris were not new to Africa when Stewart Edward White explored the Serengeti in 1913. Four years earlier, after Theodore Roosevelt completed his second term as US president, he and his son Kermit went on safari in East Africa. They went to collect specimens for the Smithsonian Institution's National Museum of Natural History in Washington, DC. There, the animals would be studied, stuffed, and placed on display for the American public. Roosevelt killed a total of 512 animals, including seventeen lions and twenty-nine zebras. He noted that he and Kermit "kept about a dozen trophies" for themselves. Roosevelt loved the excitement of the hunt. "It made our veins thrill," he wrote.

CHAPTER 8
Serengeti Shall Not Die

To protect the shrinking lion population in the Serengeti, the British colonial government established a small, eight-hundred-acre game reserve in 1921. It was expanded in 1929. Hunting, fishing, camping, cutting trees, and burning grass became illegal.

Outside the game reserve, laws were introduced to regulate hunting. Poisoned arrows, nets, traps, and snares were outlawed. Guns were still permitted, but hunters had to buy game licenses.

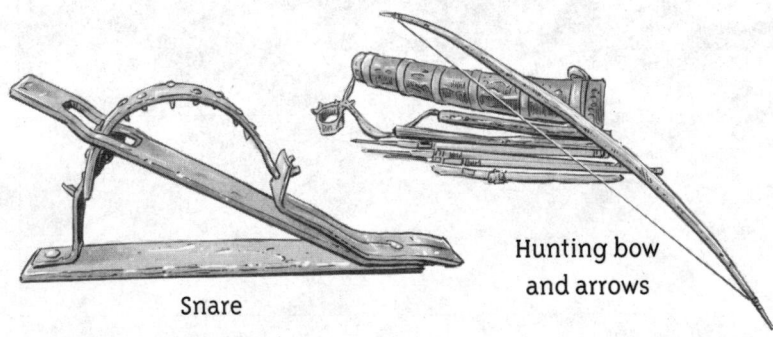

Snare

Hunting bow
and arrows

These rules basically made it so that only wealthy white colonists and foreign tourists could hunt the local wildlife.

Many of the former white hunters became game wardens. Their duty now was to protect the Serengeti's wildlife. Some came to believe that their old ways had been destructive. They became outspoken champions for the conservation movement.

In 1951, Serengeti National Park was established. This protected an even larger area from human settlement and hunting. However, more than seven thousand people—including the Maasai—and one hundred thousand cattle were already living within the boundaries of the new park. What would happen to them?

The Maasai wanted to continue to graze their livestock on their ancestral lands. But conservationists wanted to protect the land for wildlife. Over the next several years, there was much disagreement among the government, park officials, and local residents about what to do.

In the late 1950s, Bernhard and Michael Grzimek, who were a father-and-son team from Germany, worked to raise awareness about the wonders of the Serengeti. They wanted the public to know why it was important to expand and protect the park for future generations.

Dr. Bernhard Grzimek was born in what is now Poland in 1909. He was put in charge of the Frankfurt Zoo in Germany in 1945. (At the end of World War II, only twelve of the zoo's animals were still alive.) Grzimek rebuilt the zoo and led it for nearly thirty years.

When Serengeti National Park was established in the 1950s, little was known about the vast migrating herds. So in 1957, Dr. Grzimek and Michael decided to count the Serengeti's herds and watch where they went. "We [intend] to make a census . . . and to plot the movements of these huge armies."

Dr. Bernhard Grzimek

The Grzimeks figured the best way to survey the area was by air. So they learned how to fly. That December, they began their six-thousand-mile journey from Germany to East Africa in a small striped plane they called their "flying zebra."

They learned that part of the Great Wildebeest Migration route lay outside the boundaries of the newly established park. They proposed redrawing some of the park's boundaries to protect the herds.

The Grzimeks published a book about their findings, called *Serengeti Shall Not Die*. In it,  they made the case that the Serengeti was a unique place that deserved to be protected. They compared the great African herds to those of the American bison before settlers nearly wiped them out. They wrote: "A hundred and fifty years ago gigantic herds of other types of animals thundered across the prairies of North America and Canada in similar abundance. . . . In the years to come you will have to fly to the Serengeti if you want to see the splendor that was nature, before God gave it to man. . . . That will be the only place to watch big herds on the move, *if* they are still moving then."

The Grzimeks were saying that if people weren't careful, the incredible African herds could meet the same fate as the American bison, which nearly went extinct in the late 1800s. They made a film about the Serengeti, and in 1960, it won an Academy Award.

A committee was established to study and redraw the park's boundaries. As for the people who lived on the wildebeests' migration route, a 1957 report from the committee stated: "Inside the boundaries we have recommended, certain human rights . . . will have to be extinguished." This meant that the people living inside the new Serengeti National Park boundaries had to leave.

It took until 1960 to force everyone from the land. Homeless, the Maasai and other local tribes had no choice but to try to rebuild their lives outside the park's borders.

The American Serengeti

One area of the Great Plains is known as America's Serengeti. Yellowstone and Grand Teton National Parks—and surrounding areas in Wyoming, Montana, and Idaho—are home to a great number of different large animal species. Cougars, bears, wolves, and coyotes hunt moose, elk, pronghorn antelope, and bighorn sheep. And where the

Serengeti has herds of wildebeests, the *American* Serengeti has herds of bison. Weighing up to two thousand pounds, the bison is the largest mammal in North America. In 2016, it was named the national mammal of the United States.

Before the 1800s and the arrival of white American settlers, there were as many as *sixty million* bison living in North America! But by 1889, due to large-scale hunting, there were barely one thousand bison left. Today, the herds are protected, and there are about thirty thousand in the wild.

American bison

Even today, Maasai herders are harassed and arrested by local officials. Their homes and villages on the outskirts of the Serengeti are being burned down to make way for luxury safari camps. The Tanzanian government denies any involvement, but the Maasai don't believe them. They continue to fight for survival.

Even with their migration route protected with the drawing of the park's new boundaries, animals in the Serengeti have continued to face threats.

In 1956, there were just eight park rangers—with one Land Rover truck—to patrol all of Serengeti National Park. Meanwhile, the human population along the western edge of the Serengeti had been growing. Well-organized groups of poachers (illegal hunters) were killing animals by the thousands for their meat and their skins. Colonel P. G. Molloy, director of Tanzania National Parks at the time, estimated that at least 150,000 animals were lost to poaching every year.

The park rangers got to work, building guard posts around the park. Over the years, more rangers were hired, and equipment began to roll in. Eventually, an airstrip was built to receive supplies and to provide a base to conduct air patrols to track poachers' movements.

The main office of the Lake Ndutu ranger post

Still, the "poaching wars" raged on.

Among the poachers' favorite weapons was the wire snare. This cruel trap tightens over the legs of any animal that steps into it. As the animal tries to escape, the snare tightens more, cutting painfully into the animal's flesh. In 1969 alone, rangers destroyed 2,715 of these snares and arrested 364 poachers.

Rangers removing a snare

Even today, the fight against poaching can seem like a losing battle. In a six-month period in 2017, more than *seven thousand* snares were removed from Serengeti National Park.

Nowadays, more than three million people live along the western edge of the Serengeti. As the area becomes more crowded with people, good-paying jobs have become harder to find. Some people have become less concerned with the survival of the Serengeti's herds than they are about feeding themselves and their families. They want to survive, too.

As a result, there is high demand for bush meat—the meat of wild animals. It's estimated that at least two hundred thousand animals are killed annually—for their meat, their hides, and in the case of elephants and rhinoceroses, for their ivory tusks and horns.

The Serengeti even faces threats from the very government that "protects" it. The Tanzanian government recently tried to build a transport road that would cut across part of the Serengeti. Luckily, the East African Court of Justice ruled against this action. It said the road would be "unlawful" because of the impact it would have on the environment.

For the most part, the Tanzanian government remains committed to conservation. One-quarter of all its land is set aside for national parks, reserves, and other protected areas.

Tourists come from all around the world to enjoy the incredible scenery and wildlife of the Serengeti. These visitors contribute millions of dollars to the local economy and to conservation efforts. They go on safari to get up close and personal with the Serengeti's animals. Some visitors explore the area from the air, just like the Grzimeks—but in hot-air balloons.

Brave park rangers continue to patrol the Serengeti in pursuit of poachers. Their work helps ensure the survival of the herds.

And just as they have for thousands of years, the great wildebeest herds continue their annual circular march, surviving by the millions, against all odds. "Only nature is eternal," the Grzimeks wrote in *Serengeti Shall Not Die*, "unless we senselessly destroy it."

Timeline of the Serengeti

mya = million years ago

500 mya	Kopje "mountain islands" form in what is now Tanzania
20 mya	Great Rift Valley forms; volcanoes spew ash over what will become the Serengeti Plain
1700s	Maasai herdsmen arrive in the Serengeti area
1890	Rinderpest outbreak reaches the Serengeti, killing much of the Maasai's livestock
1891	Austrian geographer Oscar Baumann maps the Serengeti
1904, 1911	Maasai people sign unfair treaties, ceding their land to British settlers
1913	American writer and hunter Stewart Edward White explores the northern Serengeti; era of big-game safari hunts begins
1919	Great Britain assumes control over Tanzania
1921	Game reserve established to protect lion population
1951	Serengeti National Park established
1957	Dr. Bernhard Grzimek and his son Michael survey the Serengeti by air
1959	The Grzimeks' book, *Serengeti Shall Not Die*, is published
1960	The last of the Maasai people removed from Serengeti National Park
1961	Tanzania becomes an independent nation
2014	East African Court of Justice rules against plans to build a road through the Serengeti

Timeline of the World

500 mya	Prehistoric animals begin leaving the water to explore land for the first time
465 mya	Plants begin to flourish on land
230 mya	Dinosaurs evolve during the Triassic period
25 mya	Tailless apes evolve from monkeys, which have tails
1707	Scotland and England join to become the United Kingdom of Great Britain on May 1
1788	English convicts brought to Australia
1890	US troops and Native Americans clash at Wounded Knee in South Dakota
1904	Guglielmo Marconi transmits a message from US president Theodore Roosevelt to England's King Edward VII; it is the first successful wireless communication between the United States and Europe
1915	Rocky Mountain National Park established
1922	Ireland becomes independent from Great Britain
1950	Korean War begins when Communist troops from the north invade the south
1959	Fidel Castro becomes the leader of Cuba
1961	Conservation group World Wildlife Fund founded
1966	Congress passes Endangered Species Preservation Act
2014	Scotland votes against independence, remains part of the United Kingdom

Bibliography

Casey, George, director. *Africa: The Serengeti.* Los Angeles: Graphic Films, 1994.

Cross, Robert. "The harmony and the hunger: Serengeti." *Chicago Tribune.* September 24, 2000, http://www.chicagotribune.com/lifestyles/travel/chi-wondersserengeti-story.html.

Grzimek, Bernhard, and Michael Grzimek. *Serengeti Shall Not Die.* Translated by E. L. and D. Rewald. London: Hamish Hamilton, Ltd., 1960.

Sinclair, Anthony R. E. *Serengeti Story: Life and Science in the World's Greatest Wildlife Region.* Oxford, England: Oxford University Press, 2012.

Turner, Myles. *My Serengeti Years: The Memoirs of an African Game Warden.* New York: W. W. Norton & Co., Inc., 1988.

Yong, Ed. "The Great Thing About Mass Wildebeest Drownings." *The Atlantic.* June 19, 2017, https://www.theatlantic.com/science/archive/2017/06/how-the-mass-drownings-of-wildebeest-feed-the-serengeti/530799/.